INSECTS
of Australia

Paul Zborowski

First published in 2020 by Reed New Holland Publishers
Sydney

Level 1, 178 Fox Valley Road, Wahroonga, NSW 2076, Australia

newhollandpublishers.com

A record of this book is held at the National Library of Australia.

All images by Paul Zborowski except the following: *Austrothemis nigrescens*,
Chasmoptera hutti, *Blepharotes corarius*, *Miltinus maculipennis*, *Medomega averyi*,
Comptosia sp., *Anisynta sphenosema* and *Hemithynnus* sp. by Jean and Fred Hort;
Apoderus coryii by Bernhard Jacobi; *Tineola bisselleilla* by Ross Schumacher/CSIRO;
and *Pieris rapae* by Shutterstock/Steve Byland.

ISBN 978 1 92554 644 6

Managing Director: Fiona Schultz
Publisher and Project Editor: Simon Papps
Designer: Andrew Davies
Production Director: Arlene Gippert
Printed in China

10 9 8 7 6 5 4 3 2

Keep up with Reed New Holland
and New Holland Publishers

 ReedNewHolland
 @ReedNewHolland

CONTENTS

Apoderus coryii

INTRODUCTION

What is an Insect?

The insects are the most successful creatures on the planet. The Animal Kingdom is divided into several large groups called Phyla. At this level, all backboned animals, for example, are in one phylum, Chordata. In terms of species numbers this is a small group. By far the largest is the phylum Arthropoda which includes the insects. This group is characterised by having an external skeleton called an exoskeleton which is composed of separate hardened plates or segments, joined by softer tissue that allows movement of these segments. This structure gives strong physical and chemical protection from the environment on the outside, and sturdy points for muscle attachment on the inside. It is such a successful formula that arthropods represent about 90 per cent of all animal species, with the insects accounting for the majority of these.

Evolution

Insects have been around since long before the dinosaurs, with the earliest known fossils dating back nearly 400 million years. The fast turnover of generations, and the vast numbers involved in each generation, provide ample opportunity for random mutations to sometimes be beneficial for survival. A gene allowing better sensory information, or longer hunting reach, or speed, is likely to prosper in further generations. Nevertheless, unless there is a strong selection pressure acting on an insect species, their form has already settled into a very amazing survival format. Cockroaches have been around, looking almost exactly the same as now, for more than 300 million years. Dinosaurs came and went during this time, and great changes in the adaptability and shapes and sizes of the higher animals have taken place. Flight also evolved that early, but the first winged insects were very large, and their wings were unable to fold to help them to hide. After several group extinctions, the modern foldaway wing forms evolved. The last major changes coincided with the evolution of flowering plants, starting about 130 million years ago. The modern insect orders of flies, wasps and moths/butterflies have expanded since, performing the mutually beneficial job of pollination. The most recently arrived group is the bees.

The Insect Body

The different classes within the arthropods have different numbers of segments and appendages. The insect body has three main divisions: the head, thorax and abdomen. The head has multi-faceted eyes, usually sideways acting jaws, or mouthparts modified for sucking or mopping up food. It has any sensory organs, especially the antennae, which is a very sensitive 'nose', and palps around the mouth form taste and manoeuvring food.

Three sets of legs and two or four wings are mounted on the thorax. Four wings are the norm, and some are all rigid, such as those of the dragonflies and butterflies. Others have toughened upper wings that serve as protective cases for the soft, larger, flying lower wings. These fold away via complex origami-like folds. The reproductive parts are at the end of the abdomen, and sometimes include an

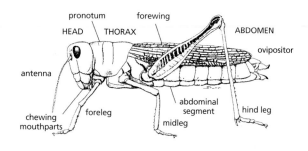

A typical adult insect illustrating the major parts of the body.

egg-laying 'tube' called an ovipositor. This structure has adapted as a stinger in some wasps and ants.

Everything is encased in the tough outer 'skeleton', a skin replacement so tough that the creatures need no internal skeleton. Because insects are very light, this armour is generally good enough to survive a fall from any height, and a lot of ritual and real fighting. The exoskeleton can also be soft, as in caterpillars, but even this is still made from the same superb protein called chitin. It is not just tough, but water resistant, so that, for instance, insects can survive in hot deserts without instantly drying up. Or can live under water. Many sensory bristles and hairs are found all over the body, and these warn of danger by sensing air movements caused by approaching objects or enemies.

The Life Cycle

Insects have evolved two different sequences of maturing. Both involve having to shed the exoskeleton periodically, as it cannot expand to accommodate growth.

A katydid cricket slowly 'walking' out of its old outer skeleton, or 'skin'. This is done at night for protection, as the new layer needs time to harden.

The older insect groups, such as cockroaches, grasshoppers and true bugs, undergo incomplete metamorphosis. Starting form egg, they hatch into tiny copies of the adult, minus reproductive organs and wings. Over many growth spurts and sheddings of the exoskeleton, they gain size, and at the last moult gain sexual maturity and wings, if present in that species. These insects tend to live the same life as immature stages and adults, feeding on the same food source in the same habitats, sometimes in groups.

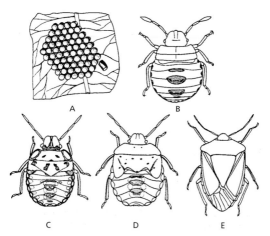

Stages in the incomplete metamorphosis life cycle illustrated by a shield bug, family **Pentatomidae** (order Hemiptera): (A) eggs; (B) first instar nymph; (C) third instar nymph with very early wing buds; (D) final instar nymph with wing sheaths; (E) the adult or imago, with full wings.

The other more recent growth pattern, complete metamorphosis, involves two different stages. Each stage potentially live completely different lives, utilising different parts of the habitat. The egg hatches into a larvae stage, usually caterpillar- or grub-like, and this stage undergoes growth moults while feeding at a great rate. When ready, these insects make a pupa or chrysalis stage, often protected by silk and hidden. Inside this 'container' they undergo a total

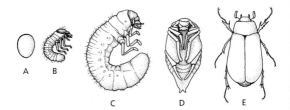

Stages in the complete metamorphosis life cycle, illustrated by a beetle, family *Scarabaeidae* (order Coleoptera): (A) egg; (B) early larval stage; (C) final larval stage; (D) the stationary pupa showing developing adult characteristics, like wing sheaths; (E) the winged adult or imago.

change of form. What emerges is the full adult, often winged stage, which then begins a different, more mobile life than the immature stage. Butterflies, flies and beetles are typical examples.

Both growth sequences start from eggs in the vast majority of cases. However, some parasitic insects, and flies, 'hatch' the egg internally and produce a free-living larvae. In these cases the number of offspring is much lower, but the young have a head start. The number of eggs from one female varies from a few, to tens of thousands in some moths. Eggs are usually laid directly on food plant leaves in herbivores, and in almost any open or hidden location for other insects. In species with an ovipositor, such as crickets and wasps, the eggs are inserted into leaves and crevices, or into prey directly. Water insects often just drop eggs into a pond, while others, such as mosquitoes, can make floating rafts.

How Insects Live

Every conceivable life strategy, and every life-possible habitat is used by the myriad forms of insects. Think of an inhospitable habitat, and chances are insects have adapted to make use of it. Hot springs, rainless deserts, snow, deep caves, underground rivers, toxic food sources, are all resources and homes to insects. The majority are either herbivores or detritivores (dead organic matter like leaf litter). Many are hunters, usually of other insects, but creatures from worms, spiders, to small vertebrates, are on the menu too. Perhaps the most important insects are the parasites, representing mainly wasps, they are responsible for greater insect population control than the hunters.

How Many Insect Species Are There?

This question has many answers. The most reliable numbers to quote are of the species that have been found by entomologists and named. Right now, across the world, more than 950,000 insect species are named. A much greater number than that have been discovered, but many are still awaiting the complicated species description and naming process. About 20,000 new species are named each year. So, about 1.5 million species have been seen and caught. And then there are the rest – the predictions. Since studies of canopy insects in tropical forests began the estimates have gone astronomical. Some studies find that 'fogging' a tree in Amazonia, which lets you see every insect there that day, results in a majority of the species being new to science. More studies have reduced this to maybe half or less, but still result in current estimates of anywhere from 2 million to 10 million insect species worldwide! For Australia these numbers are about 65,000 species named, and about 200,000 estimated to exist.

It is sad to contemplate that habitat destruction, especially in the tropics, will result in the majority of invertebrate species never even being seen by humans before we force them into extinction.

The Australian Insect Fauna

Australia split from the Gondwana supercontinent between about 200 million and 160 million years ago. Before that, Antarctica, Australia, Africa and South America had no borders and insects evolved over the large land mass together. After the split, each continent provided its own evolutionary pressures on the insects. Even today, many groups can be seen to be similar, especially between Australia and southern South America. Fossils in Antarctica show that it had these insect groups also, until it drifted too far south to be hospitable. Relatively recently Australia had several land bridges to South-East Asia via New Guinea, but as the continent dried to its current state, many insects have adapted for desert conditions, rather than the wet tropical habitats of South-East Asia.

Classification

All living things have been classified by a 'binomial' system, which means 'with two names', since the days of Carl Linnaeus in the mid-18th century. He ordered the most similar organisms into genera, and the individual species within that genus have a unique species name. So, for example, *Pieris* is a genus of white butterflies with about 40 species. The best known is *Pieris rapae*, the Cabbage White. The genus *Pieris* belongs to a family of similar butterflies, known as Pieridae, 'the whites'. It in turn is part of the large order of insects, the Lepidoptera, which means 'scale winged' and therefore all the butterflies and moths. Currently there are about 26 orders of insects. Taxonomists, the scientists who classify life, often make changes even at this high level. Recently, due to new evolutionary findings, the cockroaches and termites were incorporated into one order from two. Above this level are all six-legged, exoskeleton-covered creatures, the insects, in the class Insecta.

Order: Lepidoptera
Family: **Pieridae**
Genus: *Pieris*
Species: *rapae*
Common name: Cabbage White butterfly

HOW TO USE THIS BOOK

With more than 65,000 species of insects already named in Australia, this pocket book is necessarily very introductory. All the insect orders – the level at which for instance beetles are separated from flies – are present. Within these orders, there are more than 660 families of insects – the level at which for example, ladybird beetles are separated from scarab beetles. Some of these families represent very few species, or insects that are very rarely seen because of their tiny size or hidden habits. Therefore the most 'seen' insect families have been chosen to represent their orders, and are organised with colour-coded tops of pages. Each major chapter, such as the one for 'beetles', starts with information on what visible features define that group, and what are the habits of the adults and immature stages. Also mentioned is the number of species found in Australia.

Each page then introduces the largest and/or better known families, such as ladybirds, with general information about size, habits, species numbers, and distribution. Family names are highlighted, while genus and species names are in italics, which is the standard in biological literature. Once you know the family of an insect, it is already possible to know something of its life history and the habits of adults and larvae. Therefore, even if only a few or even one species per family may fit in this pocket-sized book, the knowledge gained is far broader.

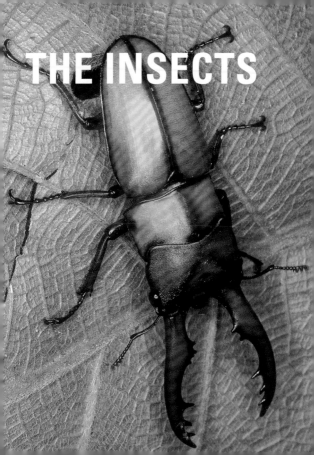

THE INSECTS

SILVERFISH Order Thysanura: 39 species

ID: Primitive wingless insects with a scaly to hairy elongate body and three long tail-like cerci. Silverfish are smaller and have smaller eyes than bristletails, while the outer cerci tend to splay out.

Ctenolepisma sp., **Lepismatidae**. The common worldwide silverfish.

HABITS: The main species are found worldwide and are minor pests in houses, others live with ants and termites.

BRISTLETAILS Order Archaeognatha: 10 species

ID: Large eyes often meet in the middle, and cerci tend to be straight (cf. Silverfish).

HABITS: Live in moist outdoor places, such as under bark and leaf litter, and in beached seaweed.

A rainforest bristletail, **Meinertellidae**, from Qld, 15mm.

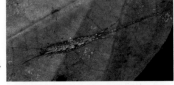

17

MAYFLIES Order Ephemeroptera: 113 species

ID: Aquatic insects. Adults elongate, with four membranous wings held together and upright at rest, head with often very large bulbous eyes and three 'tails' (cerci) held apart.

HABITS: Common along fresh upland streams, where they sometimes have perform mating flights in densely packed groups and do not feed during a very short adult life.

Atalophlebia sp., **Leptophlebiidae**. Nymphs found in clear streams and lakes, with three 'tails' (cerci) and hair-like gills on the sides of the body. Feed on algae and detritus from one to several years.

A typical mayfly nymph, *Atalophlebia* sp., **Leptophlebiidae**, with hair-like gills along the sides.

DRAGONFLIES AND DAMSELFIES
Order Odonata: 325 species

DRAGONFLIES

ID: Aquatic insects. Adults have four hard complex-veined wings – usually transparent, sometimes coloured – which are held out flat at rest, large spherical eyes and chewing mouthparts. The aquatic nymphs are flattened, a large head has mouthparts which shoot forward to catch prey, and three small pointed gills at the rear.

HABITS: Adults are fast acrobatic hunters of flying insects, nymphs hunt aquatic insects, tadpoles, and even small fish. Males defend a flying territory and court females which enter.

Scarlet Percher, *Diplacodes haematodes,* **Libellulidae**. Male. Australia-wide.

Red Swampdragon, *Agrionoptera insignis*, **Libellulidae**. From Qld and NT.

Iridescent Flutterer, *Rhyothemis braganza*, **Libellulidae**. From Qld, NT and Kimberleys.

Swamp Flat-tail, *Austrothemis nigrescens*, **Libellulidae**. Occurs from coastal NSW to WA.

Typical dragonfly nymph, underwater.

DAMSELFLIES

ID: More slender versions of dragonflies, with membranous see-through wings usually held together, upright, at rest. Very large eyes protruding sideways from a small head. The aquatic larvae also more dainty than dragonflies, and with characteristic three leaf-like gills at the rear end.

HABITS: Adults and nymphs are hunters of other insects, often beneficial as damsels by preying on the likes of mosquitoes.

Common Bluetail, *Ischnura heterosticta*, **Coenagrionidae**. Male feeding on another damsel. Found all over Australia.

Common Bluestreak, *Lestoidea conjuncta*, **Lestoideidae**. Male. From Qld.

Typical damselfly nymph, underwater.

Tropical Rockmaster, *Diphlebia euphoeoides,* **Diphlebiidae**. Male. One of the largest Australian species, from the Qld coast.

STONEFLIES Order Plecoptera: 196 species

ID: Adult 10–40mm long, nymph up to 60mm. Adult flattened with four membranous wings, with strong venation patterns and often dark colour, held flat on top of the body at rest. Two 'tails' (cerci) at the end, short in adults, and about half body length in the aquatic nymphs, which have small gill tufts mainly under the abdomen.

HABITS: Nymphs live in clear waters feeding mainly on algae and detritus and some are predators, taking from a few months to three years to mature. Adults live near steams, especially in high country.

Above: Stonefly, *Dinotoperla* sp., **Gripopterygidae**. 18mm. Eastern Australia.

Right: Stonefly nymph.

COCKROACHES Order Blattodea: 535 species

ID: Adults 3–70mm long. Flattened, broad body, with long, many-segmented, thin antennae and usually slender legs adapted for running. Some wingless, but most with two pairs of wings, the upper pair forming a leathery toughened shield over the membranous rear wings at rest. Eggs are laid into a characteristic leathery 'bag' and the nymphs look like small wingless adults.

HABITS: The majority of species are detritus eaters in the wild, mainly nocturnal, living under bark or stones or in leaf litter. Only a few species have adapted to life in houses and gained pest status. Some live with ants and termites.

Cosmozosteria maculimarginata, **Blattidae**. Female of a wingless species from Qld interior.

Laxta granicollis, **Blebaridae**. A wingless female (males winged). Found under bark in NSW and Qld.

Golden Cockroach, *Ellipsidion australe,* **Ectobiidae**. Active in daytime on leaves. Common from Vic to NT.

Giant Burrowing Cockroach, *Macropanesthia rhinoceros*, **Blaberidae**. Found in eastern NSW and Qld, in sandy soils where it lives in family groups which care for the young.

Australian Cockroach, *Periplaneta australasiae,* **Blattidae**. Although probably introduced, now occurs all over the country as a pest in houses. Note the egg sac, called an ootheca, it is carrying behind it.

TERMITES Order Blattodea: 350 species

ID: 3–18mm long. Termites are soft, usually cream-coloured insects, with no functional eyes, short antennae, and mouthparts either with mandibles, or adapted into a turret for spraying a glue-like substance. Divided into castes; workers of different sizes, soldiers, a queen, and a male caste periodically produced for starting new nests.

HABITS: Along with the bees and ants, these are the most socially organised insects, living in colonies up to a million strong with giant

nests above ground or underground. Clever design allows the nests to be temperature steady and highly humid. Termites forage at night for grass, wood and other plant matter, sometimes building earth tunnels to escape predation.

Nest of Spinifex Termite, *Nasutitermes triodiae*, **Termitidae**. Common across tropical north from Qld to WA.

Nest of *Nasutitermes walkeri*, **Termitidae** – a tree species from the east coast.

Spinifex Termite soldier, *Nasutitermes triodiae*, **Termitidae**. A 'nasute' species with a glue-spraying turret head.

Ringant Termite, *Neotermes insularis*, **Kalotermitidae**. Soldier and workers of the largest termite in Australia, found in Eucalypt forests from NT and along the east to Vic.

MANTIDS Order Mantodea: 160 species

ID: 10–120mm long. Elongate body, with raptorial toothed front legs adapted for grabbing prey. Four wings, with upper pair forming a leathery cover for the more delicate lower membranous pair. A few species are wingless, and some are ground-runners mimicking ants. Head somewhat triangular, very mobile, with large eyes and chewing mandibles.

HABITS: Mantids are all hunters, as nymphs and adults, slowly stalking insect prey using acute vision to zero in. Eggs are laid into a frothy covering called an ootheca, and the nymphs take several months to mature.

Green Mantis, *Orthodera ministralis*, **Mantidae**. The common green mantis over most of Australia.

Hooded Horror, *Hierodula atricoxis,* **Mantidae**. At 100mm one of the largest mantids. From north Qld.

Net-winged Mantis, *Neomantis australis,* **Mantidae**, from the tropics.

Phthersigena sp., **Amorphoscelidae**. Part of a group of ground-running species, with wingless females.

Gyromantis sp., **Amorphoscelidae**. One of several species common on tree trunks around Australia.

EARWIGS Order Dermaptera: 85 species

ID: 5–50mm. Elongate insects with pincer-like structures at the rear. Short forewings form leathery covers for complex membranous wings cleverly folded under them.

HABITS: Omnivorous, feeding mainly on plant matter, but dead and living insects too. Some burrow, but most live under wood and stones.

Male European Earwig, *Forficula auricularia*, **Forficulidae**. An introduced species found all over temperate Australia.

Native earwig, *Chelisoches* sp., **Chelisochidae**, from eastern Australia.

CRICKETS AND GRASSHOPPERS
Order Orthoptera: 1,500 species

CRICKETS

ID: 5–100mm. Elongate insects with enlarged rear legs, long thin, more than 30-segmented antennae, and a curved sword-like egg-laying organ, ovipositor, at the rear of the females, used to insert eggs into crevices. Most winged, with forewings leathery, protecting the larger membranous hindwings.

HABITS: Crickets can be herbivorous, but many are hunters, some with enlarged mandibles. The majority are nocturnal and many nocturnal insect songs are produced by crickets, mainly by rubbing a file on one front wing on a different file on the other one.

The common black field cricket, *Teleogryllus* sp., **Gryllidae**. Sings loudly in open country all over Australia.

Euscyrtus hemelytrus, **Gryllidae**, a common grass cricket in NSW and Qld.

A typical wood cricket, *Hyalogryllacris* sp., **Gryllacrididae**.

The badly named 'long-horned grasshopper', *Conocephalus semivittatus*, **Tettigoniidae**, is actually a common day-active katydid – a cricket.

Humpbacked Katydid, *Elephantodeta* sp., **Tettigoniidae**. A common green katydid species.

A widespread katydid, *Torbia* sp., **Tettigoniidae**.

GRASSHOPPERS

ID: 5–80mm. Elongate insects with very enlarged rear legs adapted for jumping. Usually winged with the forewings leathery, covering larger membranous hindwings. No sword-like ovipositor in the females, and antennae short and less than 30-segmented.

HABITS: All are herbivores, eating mainly grasses and leaves with short but very strong mandibles. Eggs usually laid underground and covered with froth. Most are diurnal and produce sound by rubbing a file on the inside of the rear leg against a file on the side of the wing.

Monistria pustulifera, **Pyrgomorphidae**. Many species of this family are either short-winged, or wingless, and wildly coloured to warn predators that they are poisonous. Found widely, but mainly inland.

41

Australian Plague Locust, *Chortoicetes terminifera,* **Acrididae**.
A serious pest of inland crops.

Opposite: Mating 'cone-head' grasshoppers, *Atractomorpha* sp.,
Pyrgomorphidae. Common all over Australia.

Yellow-winged Locust, *Locusta migratoria*, **Acrididae**. A seasonal pest in northern Australia.

One of the toad or rock grasshoppers, *Raniliela* sp., **Acrididae**. Found in the stony deserts of central Australia.

One of the 'monkey grasshoppers', *Biroella* sp., **Eumastacidae**, which sit with rear legs splayed out sideways. Qld.

STICK INSECTS AND LEAF INSECTS
Order Phasmida (Phasmatodea): 105 species

ID: 30–300mm long. Usually long and cylindrical with long thin legs and cryptic green or brown colours. If winged, often with short forewings forming a cover for larger membranous wings, which sometimes have colour that may startle a predator.

HABITS: All are herbivores, using cryptic stick and bark patterns to hide during the day and feed mainly at night on shrub and tree foliage. Eggs are often seed mimics and are scattered randomly.

Anchiale briareus, **Phasmatidae**. Short-winged stick insect in threat display, eastern Australia, 160mm.

Macleay's Spectre, *Extatosoma tiaratum*, **Phasmatidae**. Our most robust species – here a 140mm wingless female, while the smaller males are winged.

Peppermint Stick Insect, *Megacrania batesii*, **Phasmatidae**. A uniquely blue coloured species which emits peppermint-like defensive smells. North Qld, 100mm.

Green stick insect, *Podacanthus* sp., **Phasmatidae**. Female from eastern Australia.

WEB-SPINNERS Order Embioptera: 26 species

ID: 4–15mm. Small, dark, elongate, short-legged insects, living in silk tunnels on and under bark. Males with four membranous wings, females wingless, and both with bulbous enlarged front tarsi, which house silk glands.

HABITS: Large family groups live gregariously in ever-expanding silk tunnels, with the longer-lived females dispersing to start new colonies, while their progeny expand existing colonies. Feed on leaves, lichen and mosses.

Australembia sp., **Australembiidae**. Wingless female web-spinner, 12mm.

Oligotomidae. A winged male web-spinner, 10mm.

49

BOOKLICE Order Psocodea (formerly Psocoptera): 300 species

ID: 1–10mm. Small to minute soft insects, often wingless, and head wider than the body. If winged, four membranous wings held tent-like over the body.

HABITS: Only a few tiny wingless species are the classic booklice, living in homes as minor pests. The majority live under bark or stones or openly in forest habitats, eating mainly plant-based detritus.

Myopsocus sp., **Myopsocidae**. Typical wingless booklouse, like the home pest species.

Sigmatoneura formosa, **Psocidae**. Typical winged booklouse.

LICE Order Psocodea (formerly Phthiraptera): 500 species

ID: 0.5–10mm. Small to minute soft, colourless insects, with flattened bodies, small to no eyes, and either biting or sucking mouthparts.

HABITS: Most species are external parasites on mammals and birds. Some live in the nests and feed on skin cells, but many live on the hosts and feed on detritus or suck blood. Most have coevolved with specific hosts, and never leave their bodies.

Human Head Louse, *Pediculus capitus,* Pediculidae, attached to hair. Found everywhere, unfortunately.

Unidentified typical bird louse, on the feathers of a brush-turkey.

TRUE BUGS, HOPPERS, SCALE INSECTS AND ALLIES Order Hemiptera: 6,000 species

Members of this order are defined by their mouthparts being fused into a beak-like sucking tool. Within this large order there are three divisions: True Bugs; Hoppers and Cicadas; and Scale Insects, Aphids and allies.

TRUE BUGS

ID: 5–80mm. The 'normal' true bugs such as stink bugs, usually winged with the forewings leathery and crossed over the rear wings at rest, often half toughened and half membranous.

HABITS: Majority are sap-suckers of living plants, and many are hunters of other insects, including on and under water. The immature stages can have different colours but are usually shaped like small wingless adults.

Plant bug, *Hyalopeplus* sp., **Miridae**. **Miridae** is the largest family of bugs, with more than 600 species of similar, mainly herbivorous species. 10mm.

53

Communal seed bugs, *Graptostethus servus*, **Lygaeidae**. One of more than 400 species of sap, fruit and seed feeders and some hunters. 12mm.

Assassin bug, *Pristhesancus* sp., **Reduviidae**. A hunter of other insects. Eastern Australia, 24mm.

'Crusader bug', *Mictis profana,* **Coreidae**. A family with enlarged back legs, known in particular for this species. 20mm.

Bed bug, *Cimex lectularis,* **Cimicidae**. Lives in large family groups, feeding on human blood at night. One of the hardest pest insects to eradicate once it establishes in a house or hotel. 6mm.

Bronze-orange Bug, *Musgraveia sulciventris*, **Tessaratomidae**. One of the stinkiest stink bugs, and a pest of citrus trees. 26mm.

Shield bug, *Lyramorpha rosea*, **Tessaratomidae**. The very red nymph of a species where the adult is a subdued grey-green. From Qld, 18mm.

Shield bug, *Catacanthus nigripes*, **Pentatomidae**. One of the most striking shield bug species in Australia. From Cape York, 18mm.

Shield bug, *Poecilometis* sp., **Pantatomidae**. One of a group of similar species of shield bugs which are common on Eucalyptus tree trunks all over Australia. 16mm.

Pond skater, *Limnogonus fossarum*, **Gerridae**, with fly prey. These bugs hunt on the surface of water bodies, finding prey by the ripples they cause, and moving fast using their long mid-legs as oars.

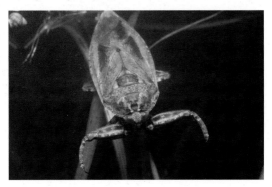

Giant fish-killer bug, *Lethocerus* sp., **Belostomatidae**. Up to 80mm long, it uses its fearsome ice tong-like front legs to grab passing water insects, tadpoles and fish.

Backswimmer, *Enithares* sp., **Notonectidae**. Very fast and slippery underwater hunter that swims upside-down with strokes of its powerful oar-like rear legs. 10mm.

HOPPERS AND CICADAS

ID: Elongate, usually winged, sap-sucking bugs. The wings are usually membranous and the forewings sit roof-like over the hindwings, along the body (not crossed over like in true bugs). The short sucking beak-like mouthparts tend to face downward, unlike the often forward-facing, longer ones, in the true bugs.

HABITS: All are plant sap-suckers. Filtering out the best sugars results in a lot of excess, still sweet, fluids ejected at the end, forming a waxy frass behind them. Ants and other insects seek them out to drink this, and protect them.

'Black Prince' cicada, *Psaltoda plaga*, **Cicadidae**, from NSW. The familiar loud call of cicadas is produced by drum skin-like tympanal organs, vibrating at high frequency, and backed by empty chambers to amplify the sound.

'Tiger Prince' cicada, *Macrotristria godingi*, **Cicadidae**, from north Qld.

Gum Tree Hopper, *Eurymeloides pulchra,* **Eurymelidae**. Adults and orange
nymphs, with attendant ants, are found all over Australia.

61

Tailed hopper nymph, **Eyrybrachyidae**. The 'antennae' are actually waxy additions – the head is at the other end, and it moves backwards to fool predators.

Aufidus sp., **Cercopidae**. Members of this family are known as a frog hoppers as adults, but the nymphs are called spittle bugs as they hide in a bubbly mess of plant juices. 10mm.

Plant hopper, *Brunotarsessus fulvus,* **Cicadellidae**. A member of the largest hopper family, with more than 700 species all over Australia. 12mm.

Tree Hopper, *Eutryonia* sp., **Membracidae**. Adults are often adorned with bizarre horns. Nymphs look completely different and often live in family groups. 10mm.

Rentinus sp., **Fulgoridae**. The fulgorid bugs are known as 'lantern bugs' for a species from South America. Many species have a horn pointing forward. 16mm.

SCALE INSECTS, APHIDS AND ALLIES

ID: These are the soft bugs. Aphids are best known, but most species of this group live hidden under wax secretions that are known as scales. Inside these many-shaped homes are little colourless 'blobs' with minute legs and a 'beak'.

HABITS: All are plant sap-suckers, often in huge numbers, which injure the plant. Many are crop and ornamental plant pests, also because their secretions attract sooty moulds which further injure the plants. In some the males emerge as flying insects, seeking the sedentary females. Most are small to minute.

Rose Aphid, *Macrosiphum rosae*, **Aphidae**. The most frequently noticed species of aphid, with many body forms, including a winged 'caste', which spreads them to new areas.

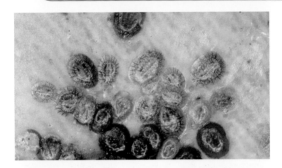

Soft Brown Scale, *Coccus hesperidum*, **Coccidae**, which afflicts mangoes. Under the wax are tiny soft insects sucking the fruit juices.

Shell scale insects, *Creils* sp., **Psyllidae**, on *Eucalyptus* leaves.

Cottony Cushion Scale, *Icerya purchasi,* **Margarodidae**. The famous pest that invaded American citrus crops, which were then saved by the introduction of an Australian ladybird beetle.

Spiralling Whitefly, *Aleurodicus dispersus,* **Aleyrodidae**. The dreaded pest of many plants, with nymphs and winged adults present.

THRIPS Order Thysanoptera: 740 species

ID: Small to minute, soft, elongate insects, often tapering to a point at the back, and with the head less wide than the body. Complex mouthparts can both rasp and suck. Wings, if present, narrow, membranous and fringed with hair.

HABITS: Some are fungus feeders, other live in flowers and eat pollen, but many are leaf and sap feeders. A number are cosmopolitan pests of crops and ornamental plants. More than 60 species in Australia are accidental pest imports.

Banana Flower Thrip, *Thrips hawaiensis,* **Thripidae**. An introduced pest. 2mm.

Mecynothrips sp., **Phlaeothripidae**. The largest Australian thrip, at 6mm long.

70

ALDERFLIES AND DOBSONFLIES
Order Megaloptera: 26 species

ID: 10–100mm. Aquatic insects with medium to large adults, with chewing mandibles and usually two pairs of large membranous wings held flat along the body. The larvae also have mandible mouthparts and gills lining both sides of the abdomen. Only four of the species are alderflies.

HABITS: Predatory aquatic larvae live in clear waters of the east coast, up to five years in cold upland streams. Adults are short lived and tend not to feed.

Archichauliodes sp., **Corydalidae**, a large dobsonfly adult from Qld, 50mm.

LACEWINGS, ANTLIONS AND MANTIS FLIES
Order Neuroptera: 600 species

ID: Skinny-bodied insects with two pairs of large complex veined wings, usually held roof- or tent-like over the body at rest. Head much broader than the body with large, often colourful patterned eyes, and short antennae, often ending in a thickened 'club'. Larvae are often flattened and have large curved jaws modified for grasping and sucking out the contents of prey.

HABITS: All larvae are predators, the antlions in their sand-pits being the most famous. Adults usually predators, although some feed on pollen. More species are found in the dry interior and the west.

Golden Lacewing, *Nymphes myrmeleonides*, **Nymphidae**. Eastern Australia, 30mm long.

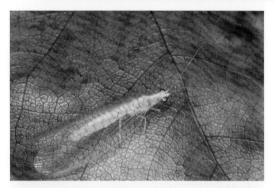

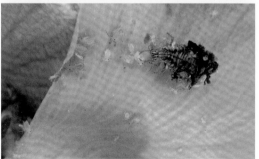

The 25mm-long classic green 'Golden-eye' Lacewing, *Mallada traviatus*, **Chrysopidae**, which is found over most of Australia, and a related nymph, hunting aphids and gluing their dead bodies onto itself for disguise.

Adult antlion, *Myrmeleon* sp., **Myrmeleontidae**, with raised wings showing the venation complexity, and the sand-pits its larvae dig to catch ants in the 'quicksand-like' effect.

Ascalaphidae is the owlfly family, with large-eyed adults and these very ferocious larvae with huge tubular jaws used for sucking out the contents of various insect prey. 10mm long.

Mantis fly, *Euclimaciella nuchalis*, **Mantispidae**. Mantis Flies are lacewings with praying mantis-like forelegs, adapted to catch, impale and grip prey. This Qld species is also known for being a general wasp mimic, giving it some protection from its own predators.

Spoonwing lacewing, *Chasmoptera hutti,* **Nemopteridae**. Most species are in the west, body only 20mm long. They have extreme rear wings, sometimes up to three times the length of the body.

BEETLES Order Coleoptera: 25,000 species

ID: The largest order of insects, characterised by the upper wings forming a tough shield, the elytra, over the lower membranous flying wings, and divided equally along the back. Mouthparts are chewing mandibles, and body shapes are very diverse.

HABITS: Virtually every lifestyle of insects, including hunters, plant eaters, scavengers, even parasites. Larvae are free living and usually have different habits to the adults.

Ground beetle, *Gnathaphanus philippensis*, **Carabidae**. A typical and common species in this family which contains more than 1,600 species. All are hunters, active mainly at night, and tend to be black and flattened, with thin legs adapted to chase down prey. This one measures 14mm, but size varies from a few mm to more than 70mm.

78

Tiger beetle, *Cicindela semicincta*, **Carabidae** (Cicindelinae). A common species of these daytime speed-hunters of the ground beetle family. They have very long legs and some can run down a fly. The head has characteristic scimitar-shaped large jaws and large bulbous eyes. Many have pretty patterns and often metallic colours, with an average size about 12mm.

Diving beetle, *Cybister* sp., **Dytiscidae**. All 270 species are aquatic hunters as larvae and adults. The beetles store air under their wing cases and can fly to find new ponds. Many new species are being discovered in fully dark underground waters. 25mm.

Whirligig beetle, *Macrogyrus elongatus*, **Gyrinidae**. Named for their crazed, fast-swimming patterns on the surface of ponds. They use the resulting waves like sonar to locate prey on the surface. Also famous for having four eyes, two for under water and two above.

Rove beetle, *Scymbalium* sp., **Staphylinidae**. A family of more than 2,000 species characterised by a very thin, elongate body, with very short wing cases, and often full-sized wings folded within. Most are black or other dark colours, from 1–22mm.

Rove beetle, *Actinus macleayi,* **Staphylinidae**. One of the largest and most colourful members of family. An active hunter, 18mm.

Burying beetle, *Diamesus osculans,* **Silphidae**. Members of this family are famous for burying small carcasses a little ball at a time, provided as food for their larvae. 25mm.

Golden Stag Beetle, *Lamprima latreillei*, **Lucanidae**, comes in many shiny hues.
This male is 25mm. Male stag beetles have these long 'jaws' used in fighting over
females.

Stag beetle, *Rhyssonotus foveolatus*, **Lucanidae**. A common species along the east
coast. 22mm. Stag beetle larvae live in soft rotting logs in wetter parts of forests.

Scarabaeidae is a family of iconic beetles that includes the Christmas beetles, chafers, elephant beetles and more. Characterised by 'lamellate' fan-like antennae. More than 2,500 species already described.

Male dung beetle, *Onthophagus ferox*, **Scarabaeidae** (Scarabaeinae), from WA, where they bury various droppings as food for their larvae. 16mm. Species from Africa have been imported to bury cattle dung here.

Christmas beetle, *Anoplognathus rugosus*, **Scarabaeidae** (Rutelinae). A typical east-coast species, 24mm. Larvae of many species feed on grass and other roots, and adults feed on leaves, especially Eucalyptus.

Christmas beetle, *Calloodes atkinsoni*, **Scarabaeidae** (Rutelinae). A large metallic species from Qld, 28mm. These and other scarab beetles commonly come to lights at houses.

Fiddler beetle or flower chafer, *Eupoecila australasiae,* **Scarabaeidae** (Cetoniinae). Common on blossom in spring over most of the country, 15mm. Flower chafers do not raise their elytra in flight, therefore the flying wings vibrate against them and cause a characteristic buzzing noise in flight.

Nectar scarab, *Phyllotocus apicallis,* **Scarabaeidae** (Melolonthinae). Common on flowers all over Australia. Species of many colours often swarm over fresh blossoms, especially those of eucalypts and their allies, and daisies. 8mm.

Elephant beetle, *Xylotrupes ulysses,* **Scarabaeidae** (Dynastinae). North Qld, 45mm. Only the males have horns.

Click beetle, *Megapenthes* sp., **Elateridae**. Members of this family are famous for a unique survival mechanism. When turned over by a predator, they use a ratchet-like structure, between the thorax and abdomen, to store tension which suddenly releases explosively, sending the beetle into a startling and loud somersault that rights it and aids escape.

Lycid beetles, *Porrostoma (Metiorrhynchus)* sp., **Lycidae**. A family of about 200 species, many of which have this brick-red colour. This advertises to predators that they taste bad. Many other more palatable insects have evolved the same colour as a mimicked protection mechanism. 16mm.

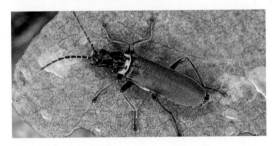

Plague Soldier Beetle, *Chauliognathus lugubris*, **Cantharidae**. Often appears in massive numbers in eastern Australia, swarming over blossom on trees and bushes. Some species in this family have protective poisons so it is best not to handle them. 15mm.

87

Firefly, *Atephylla* sp., **Lampyridae**. Fireflies are unmistakable beetles after dark, when the light-producing organs on the abdomen produce cold chemical light, which is used to attract a mate. Sixteen species are found mainly in wet forests of the east coast. 12mm.

Larvae of a carpet beetle, *Dermestes* sp., **Dermestidae**, on wool fibres. 10mm. Belongs to a family with several famous pests, including the specimen-eating museum beetles, larder beetles and hide beetles.

Clerid beetles, *Eleale* sp., **Cleridae**. A family of about 400 species of mainly hunting beetles, both as adults and larvae. Some are secretive, but many have bright metallic colours and are common on flowers in spring and summer. 14mm.

Metallic Jewel Beetle, *Selagis (Curis) caloptera*, **Buprestidae**. One of more than 1,400 species of very colourful beetles found on flowers, especially during spring. Larvae feed on roots of trees and shrubs, and adults range from 3–65mm.

Jewel beetle, *Temognatha variabilis*, **Buprestidae**. One of the larger jewel beetles found mainly on eucalypt blossom in the east. 40mm.

Jewel beetle, *Metaxymorpha gloriosa*, **Buprestidae**. This aptly named and rare species is from north Qld. 45mm.

Common Spotted Ladybird, *Harmonia (Leis) conformis,* **Coccinellidae**. One of about 500 species of these hunting beetles which are useful in our gardens. Their prey, as adults and larvae, are soft insects such as aphids. 10mm.

Striped Ladybird, *Micraspis furcifera,* **Coccinellidae**. A ferocious hunter of aphids, here on a rose. 6mm.

Darkling beetle, *Toxicum* sp., **Tenebrionidae**. The large darkling beetle family has more than 1,600 species. This species is typically shaped for this family, and lives hidden under bark and logs, eating detritus. 12mm.

Aethyssius sp., **Tenebrionidae** (Alleculinae). This subfamily of darkling beetles used to be treated as a separate family, and is characterised by this elongate shape and often very deep metallic colours. They can be found on blossom in spring. 15mm.

Piedish beetle, *Pterohealeus* sp., **Tenebrionidae**. One of a group of darkling beetles living under bark, logs and stones in the drier parts of Australia. 18mm.

Fig Longicorn, *Batocera boisduvali*, **Cerambycidae** (Lamiinae). The largest longicorn beetle in Australia,from far north Qld. The genus has many huge species through South-East Asia, with antennae sometimes three times as long as the body. 70mm.

Longicorn beetle, *Penthea pardalis,* **Cerambycidae** (Lamiinae). A striking species which breeds in acacia along the warmer parts of the east coast. 22mm.

Tiger Longicorn, *Aridaeus thoracicus,* **Cerambycidae** (Cerambycinae). Longicorn beetles are distinguished by very long antennae, which originate from the edges of the eyes. More than 1,400 species are often strongly patterned or coloured. 15mm.

Longicorn beetle, *Phoracantha (Coptocercus) trimaculatus,* **Cerambycidae** (Cerambycinae). The genus Phoracantha has many species of these brown patterned longicorns which breed in branches of eucalypts. All longicorn larvae tunnel in living and dead wood. 22mm.

Pintail or fish beetle, *Hoshihananomia* sp., **Mordellidae.** There are about 140 species of these smooth, tailed insects, which are very fast and very slippery. Found in flowers, 10mm.

Chrysomelidae are the leaf beetles – a family with more than 2,300 species of plant eaters. They come in many diverse shapes and every possible colour. The larvae, also leaf feeders, are found on the same plants, sometimes communally. Sizes from 1–30mm, averaging about 8–10mm.

Leaf beetle, *Paropsis obsoleta*, **Chrysomelidae** (Chrysomelinae). The leaf beetles most commonly seen on eucalypt and acacia leaves are the dome-shaped members of the Paropsis group. There are hundreds of species, with the larvae exuding cyanide-laced defensive fluids. 12mm.

Leaf beetle, *Paropsisterna intacta,* **Chrysomelidae** (Chrysomelinae). Another member of this domed group of leaf beetles, on eucalypt leaves. 15mm.

Spiny Leaf Beetle, *Hispellinus multispinosus,* **Chrysomelidae** (Cassidinae). Only 8mm long, but has a coat of quite sharp protective spines. Found Australia-wide.

Leaf beetle, *Colasposoma sellatum*, **Chrysomelidae** (Eumolpinae). One of the most metallic leaf beetles, from Qld, 12mm.

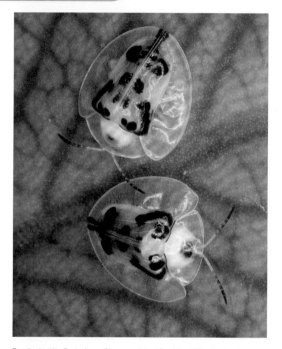

Tortoise beetle, *Emdenia* sp., **Chrysomelidae** (Cassidinae). Tortoise beetles are a very distinctive group of leaf beetles. The wing covers are expanded beyond the margin of the body, and are often transparent. Most are brightly coloured like this species from Qld. 12mm.

The Weevils, **Curculionidae**, are the most successful group of organisms on the planet, with more than 8,000 species in Australia alone. Something about their tough armoured body, with the mouthparts on the end of a 'rostrum', has contributed to this huge speciation. Most are either wood, leaf or seed feeders, with the larvae burrowing in these mediums. Sizes from 1–60mm.

Botany Bay Diamond Weevil, *Chrysolopus spectabilis*, **Curculionidae**. Not only one of the most spectacular weevils, but famous for being the first insect discovered and named in Australia, during Captain Cook's first voyage to Botany Bay, NSW. 18mm.

101

Weevil, *Othorhinchus cylindrirostris*, **Curculionidae**. The species name literally means 'with a cylindrical rostrum'. The long rostrum is very prominent in this common species, which is found over most of Australia. 20mm.

Maize Weevil, *Sitophilus zeamais*, **Curculionidae**. One of a group of worldwide pests which damage stored products such as corn, flour and other grains. They are, however, in a vast minority among the many other harmless weevils.

Weevil, *Catasarcus carbo*, **Curculionidae**. One of the many weevils which live on the ground, some of which have lost the power of flight and live long lives in cold places. Others, like this one, are fast runners protected by spines. From WA, 10mm.

Leaf-roller weevil, *Euops* sp., **Attelabidae**. Here the long-legged male has mated with the female, who is cutting the leaf half off, then rolling it with an egg inside. The larvae eat the leaf from inside out.

Brentid weevil, *Baryrhynchus* sp., **Brentidae**. A family of elongate to very
skinny weevils, with straight antennae. True weevils have the antennae bent, or
'elbowed', about in the middle. This species from Qld, 20mm.

104

STYLOPIDS Order Strepsiptera: 50–160 species

ID: This small order has very odd-looking adults. The males have the forewings reduced to 'clubs' and the hindwings very broad and large. Antennae are multi-branched. The females stay larviform, and live inside other insects which stylopids parasitise. All are minute, about 3mm being average, and rarely seen.

HABITS: Typical hosts are bugs, wasps and bees. Many species are still unnamed in museums.

Stylopid, *Triozocera* sp., **Corioxenidae**. One of the species which specialise in parasitising insects such as stink bugs (**Pentatomidae**). The females partly expose themselves between body segments of the bugs, so the flying males, like this one, can find and mate with them.

SCORPION FLIES AND HANGING FLIES
Order Mecoptera: 30 species

ID: A small group of long-legged hunting insects, a bit reminiscent of crane flies, but with strong mandibles on the end of protruding mouthparts.

HABITS: The hanging flies hang under thin branches and catch prey with modified spiny tarsi ('feet'). Larvae are free living in leaf litter and mainly scavenge for dead insects, although most adults are active hunters. The name comes from highly modified male sexual parts in some species which look like the tail-end of a scorpion.

Hanging flies, *Harpobittacus* sp., **Bittacidae**, spend their lives hanging in ambush for passing insect prey. At mating time the males catch prey to present to the females – here a very small prey is offered. In WA, 25mm each.

106

FLEAS Order Siphonaptera: 90 species

ID: Fleas are all very similar, having evolved a body extremely well suited to the task of living as external parasites on mainly furred animals. They have a very armour-plated, sideways-flattened body, which is capable of being dislodged by mammalian claws and not harmed.

HABITS: The jump mechanism is second to none – a special energy-storing muscle ratchets up pressure and locks it in place in the rear legs. When suddenly released, the force is enough to propel the flea 50 times its length, with an acceleration that would kill the best human astronaut.

Larvae are worm-like and live in the nests of the hosts, while the adults drink the host's blood directly with rasping mouthparts. The famous 'black death' epidemic in Europe in the Middle Ages was transmitted between rats and humans by rat fleas.

Dog Flea, *Ctenocephalides canis*, **Pulicidae**, on human host. Most species are dependent on single host species, although a few can switch between different ones.

FLIES Order Diptera: 8,600 species

ID: Flies are defined by the scientific name of their order, which means 'two wings'. True flies have a normal membranous pair of forewings, but the hindwings have been reduced over time to a set of club-like structures called halteres. These act as gyroscopes to further aid the amazing flight acrobatics of flies. Their mouthparts are very diverse. The majority, like the typical housefly types, have a mop-like structure that spits out saliva and mops up the mix. Biting flies have rasping rough 'beaks'.

HABITS: Fly larvae are maggots, mostly very simple, legless, soft worm-like, often living in dank or liquid places, from water itself, to dead bodies. Several families are parasites. Sizes vary from 1–70mm.

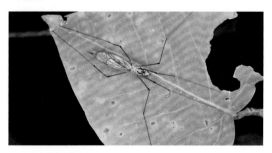

Crane flies, *Nephrotoma* sp., **Tipulidae**, share the name 'daddy-long-legs' with the skinny spiders in our homes. Most are skinny and long legged, and are the most diverse family in Australia with more than 700 species. Larvae live in wet rotting vegetation or underwater. 20mm long.

Malaria mosquito, *Anopheles farauti,* **Culicidae**. There are more than 300 species of mosquitoes in Australia, with the majority within three distinct genera, with their own co-evolved potential diseases to carry. *Anopheles* can carry malaria mainly, although in Australia the malaria parasite was eradicated after WWII.

Dengue mosquito, *Aedes aegypti,* **Culicidae**. The genus *Aedes* has the most species, and is roughly characterised by a body which ends in a point rather than rounded. Some species carry viral diseases such as Dengue, Zika and Chikungunya, and this species, which lives around all the world's warmer parts, can carry them all.

Common Banded Mosquito, *Culex annulirostris*, **Culicidae**. Belongs to the Culex genus, some species of which, such as this one, can carry the encephalitis group of viruses, Ross River virus, and other diseases. However most species of Culex, and other mosquitoes, are not carriers of any disease, and do not even bite humans.

'Sand-fly', *Culicoides* sp., **Ceratopogonidae**. This dreaded 2mm-long insect is more accurately named a biting midge. There are more than 1,000 species worldwide, including the infamous Scottish Highland Midge. They breed in wet soil on the edges of fresh and salt water, and make places like mangrove swamps impossible to survive in. Like mosquitoes, the females drink blood to feed egg production.

Midge, *Microtendipes* sp., **Chironomidae**. The word 'midge' applies to several families of flies, some very similar to mosquitoes, although with one obvious difference – they never have the long stabbing mouthparts of mozzies. Chironomids, with 200 species, are the largest group, and they rarely interact with humans. Most have aquatic larvae, including the 'bloodworms' known to fishermen.

Moth fly, **Psychodidae**. Tiny insects which often go noticed in bathrooms, as they breed in the sort of stagnant waters found in drains. Unlike moths, their shaggy coat is made of hair rather than scales. 5mm across.

Bibionid fly, *Placia ornaticornis*, **Bibionidae**. A small group of sometimes colourful flies, also called 'love-bugs', noticed mainly for their habit of staying in a mating position seemingly all day. Their larvae are known as garden maggots and are found in compost. 12mm.

March fly or horse fly, *Tabanus defilippi*, **Tabanidae**. They appear in Europe around March, in the northern spring, so March fly is a poor name for Australia. Here they appear in our spring and summer and are most pesky in higher places. Their large, wide, raspy mouthparts hurt during the bite, as they scrape through the skin to find blood, rather than inject a needle like mozzies. 20mm.

112

March fly, *Scaptia auriflua,* **Tabanidae**. Not all March flies bite humans, and not all are drab coloured. Scaptia is a genus with many colourful species, often seen on flowers. 14mm.

Soldier fly, *Hermetica illucens,* **Stratiomyidae**. The common soldier fly and its armoured maggot larvae, often found in compost bins. This family of about 90 species has a variety of larval types, most living in very rich decomposing plant matter. Adult 14mm, larva 18mm.

Robber fly, *Maira (Laphria)* sp., **Asilidae**. A dark species of robber fly from Qld, 18mm.

Robber fly, *Ommatius mackayi*, **Asilidae**. This family has about 650 species of fast-flying aerial hunters. An enlarged domed thorax has strong flying muscles, and the legs have many spines with which to hold onto prey caught on the wing. 25mm.

Mydid fly, *Miltinus maculipennis*, **Mydidae**. A small family of spectacular species, often mimicking wasps. Their larvae are mostly predators and live up to three years, while the adults have short lifespans and are often seen on flowers in arid zones. WA, 18mm.

Giant Robber Fly, *Blepharotes corarius,* **Asilidae**. One the largest flies in Australia, from WA. Body alone 32mm long.

Stiletto fly, *Medomega averyi,* **Therevidae**. Members of the therevid family, of about 110 species, are known as stiletto flies, although their often formidable-looking mouthparts are only used for digging in flowers. Larvae are mostly predators. WA, 15mm.

Bee fly, *Comptosia* sp., **Bombyliidae**. Beautiful hairy to downy flies seen at flowers or hovering over sandy soils. Some actually pick up sand and coat their eggs with it to help disguise them on the ground. 30mm wingspan.

Bee fly, *Meomyia sericans*, **Bombyliidae**. There are about 400 bee fly species in Australia. This is a fluffy species which is common in sandy shrubland inland. Body 12mm.

Long-legged fly, *Austrosciapus* sp., **Dolichopodidae**. Brightly metallic flies with delicate long legs. They are hunters, and tend to stay on the same territorial leaves during the daytime. Around 320 species in Australia. 12mm wingspan.

Hover fly, *Melangyna* sp., **Syrphidae**. Hover flies are busy pollinators, and many species hover more than they land or travel around. So this view is the most frequent one of this common species. 15mm wingspan.

Hover fly, *Austalis* sp., **Syrphidae**. Yellows dominate among the 170 species of hover flies, but there are exceptions. Most species have large and often colourful eyes. 12mm.

Hover fly, *Eristalis tenax*, **Syrphidae**. Many hover flies generally or specifically mimic wasps and bees for protection. This species is an accidental import from Europe, where it mimics the honey bee. 12mm.

Lauxaniid fly, *Cerastocara* sp., **Lauxaniidae**. This family has more than 400 species of small, varied, interestingly patterned flies, which are found in every habitat. Little is known about them. Larvae feed on rotting vegetation and some adults are associated with fungi. 6mm.

Lauxaniid fly, *Poecilohetarus* sp., **Lauxaniidae**, with bold patterns from Qld. 5mm.

Broad-mouthed fly, *Lamprogaster imperialis,* **Platystomatidae**. The broad-mouthed flies are a family of 240 species of large-headed flies often associated with fruit as adults. Larvae feed on decaying matter and some are egg predators. 9mm.

Hammerhead fly or antler fly, *Achias australis*, **Platystomatidae**. A distinctive platystomatid fly of north Qld, where the males have their eyes on the extended ends of the head, and even fight with these over females, like deer do with antlers. 12mm.

Queensland Fruit Fly, *Bactrocera tryoni*, **Tephritidae**. One of the classic orchard pests among the flies. This family of 135 species also has several introduced pest species, which include the dreaded Papaya Fruit Fly, which was eradicated by a massive effort by the Qld government.

Mediterranean Fruit Fly or Med Fly, *Ceratitis capitata,* **Tephritidae**. A serious pest of a wide variety of fruit. Invaded Australia more than 100 years ago, and has been eradicated in the east since about 1950, now present only in WA.

Stilt-legged fly, *Mimegralla* sp., **Micropezidae**. Part of a family of only 18 species of these odd, slightly ant-shaped flies which spend their time on territorial flat leaves in wet forests. Qld, 14mm.

Vinegar fly, *Drosophila* sp., **Drosophilidae**. Also known as Drosophila flies, these are the clouds of tiny insects which hover around fruit bowls. They are rotting fruit specialists, and are famous for being the main animal species used in genetic research for decades now. 4mm.

Bushfly, *Musca vetustissima*, **Muscidae**. This is THE bushfly – the species which Burke and Wills first called the 'sticky fly'. It is the scourge of the outback, made worse with the introduction of cattle. Their need for moisture makes them probe eyes, mouths, noses and ears. Australia-wide, 8mm.

Western Golden-haired Blowfly, *Calliphora albifrontalis*, **Calliphoridae**. This family of 140 species contains some useful species which aid decomposition, like this one on a dead emu, as well as some less-than-savoury types, such as the sheep blowfly.

Yellow-headed blowfly, *Amenia* sp., **Calliphoridae**. Among the members of the blowfly family which can be unpleasant, are some species that are very pretty. This one rivals many flies for colour, and its larvae are parasites of land snails. Australia-wide, 10mm.

Flesh fly, *Sarcophaga* sp., **Sarcophagidae**. The 70 species of flesh flies, like the blowflies, are major decomposers in many habitats. They differ in general appearance by the often-present three dark stripes along the top of their thorax. Larvae feed on carrion and faeces. Australia-wide, 12mm.

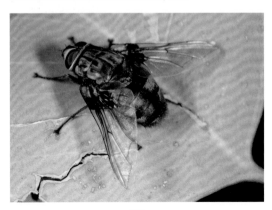

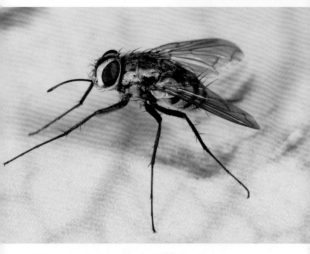

Tachinid fly, *Prosena* sp., **Tachinidae**. This long-legged tachinid fly has larvae which parasitise scarab beetles. The long 'beak' is used only for its pollination activity. 12mm.

Opposite: Tachinid fly, *Prodiaphania* sp., **Tachinidae**. Tachinids, with more than 550 species, are a major family of parasitic flies. They parasitise many moths, butterflies, beetles and more, mostly as larvae and then hatch out as the victim reaches the pupa stage. Adults are often broad, and have many erect bristles. 16mm.

Bat fly, *Cyclopodia* sp., **Nicterbiidae**. The bat flies are a very small group of external parasites which live only on bats, especially on the larger fruit bats. They have lost wings and evolved thick armour and strong large claws to stick to the fur – if they fall off, their life is over. 6mm.

CADDISFLIES Order Trichoptera: 840 species

ID: Adults are four-winged flying insects with thin long antennae and tiny chewing mouthparts. Some are hairy and even scaly, but differ from moths (which are closely related) because they lack the curled proboscis.

HABITS: Caddisflies are famous for their aquatic larvae, which build cases of many intricate designs, made from leaves, sticks or sand.

Caddisfly, *Stenopsychodes* sp. **Stenopsychidae**. The majority of species are brown to fawn in colour, although some are more bold, such as this species from Qld. Body 20mm.

Caddisfly, *Macrostemum* sp., **Hydropsychidae**. A species with typical shape and colour from the east coast. Most species prefer cool clear streams. Body 25mm.

Two examples of caddisfly larvae cases. Left: *Triplectides* sp., **Leptoceridae**, which uses leaves of various shapes and sizes. Right: a sand builder that uses silk to glue the grains, which in some species are arranged like a snail shell.

MOTHS AND BUTTERFLIES Order Lepidoptera: 10,800 species described

ID: A simple order to describe, as most have scaly wings and a curled proboscis which extends into flowers for a sugar feed. The larvae are classic caterpillars from inch-worms to hairy monsters and some serious crop pests like the cut-worms. A huge variety exists among the 93 different families, and the butterflies are merely about six distinct families of day-flying 'moths'. Other day fliers, not called butterflies, generally lack the 'clubbed' antennae of butterflies.

HABITS: Caterpillars sometimes eat poisonous plants and store the poisons to protect themselves and the adult phase, warning predators with garish colours.

MOTHS

Ghost moth, *Aenetus mirabilis*, **Hepialidae**. The Ghost moths are splendid showy large moths, which are a favourite of collectors. Their caterpillars burrow in mainly living wood for years and emerge for only a short time. This is a primitive family, which has not evolved a functional proboscis. Wingspan 140mm.

Fairy moth, *Nemophora* sp., **Adelidae**. These tiny spectacularly coloured day-flying moths flit between blossoms in the summer. 6mm long.

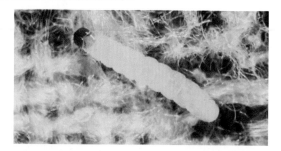

Clothes Moth, *Tineola bisselleilla,* **Tineidae**. A serious domestic pest worldwide, feeding on clothes and carpets made of natural fibres. The rest of the **Tineidae** family – more than 440 species – are largely harmless bush dwellers.

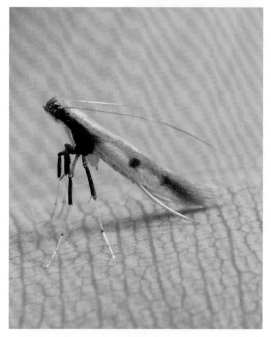

Leaf-blotch miner moths, *Caloptilia* sp., **Gracillariidae**. Part of a family of about 450 species of small, rarely noticed moths. Their larvae tunnel inside leaves leaving tell-tale raised 'blotches' in their wake, and the adults, often colourful, are distinguished by their very upright stance. 6mm long.

Case moth, *Lepidoscia* sp. **Psychidae**. The 200 or so species of case moths are famous for the many silk-glued leaf and stick homes their caterpillars shelter in. *Lepidoscia* uses straight sticks, but in other genera log cabin style, many different leaf styles, and even silk pointy bag styles abound. Shelter 30mm, adult 15mm.

Flower moth, *Glyphipterix* sp., **Glyphipterigidae**. The 60 species of flower moths would not be noticeable except that they are one of the day-flying moth families, prominent on flowers. Most are about 6–8mm long. They differ from butterflies by having antennae that come to a point, not thickened at the end, and by folding their wings close to the body when at rest.

139

Oecophoridae is the largest moth family in Australia, with more than 5,000 species. Something about the Australian bush habitat, the dry leaf litter especially, has allowed this amazing speciation of moths, whose caterpillars are mostly dead-leaf eaters. These hide in silk-joined leaf shelters. Other species feed on marsupial scat or bird scat.

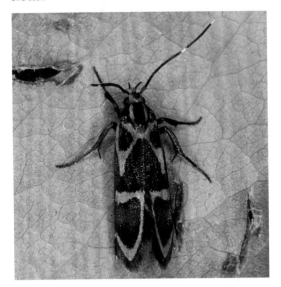

Psedaegeria phlogina, from the tropical north, 14mm long.

Euchaetis sp., from WA, 9mm long.

Habroscopa iriodes, from east-coast rainforests, 12mm long.

Oxythecta hieroglyphica, from Qld and NSW, breeds in wallaby scats, 8mm.

Ardozyga chiniprora, **Gelechiidae**. The Gelechiids are more than 800 species of diverse small moths, often elongate with wings tightly around. Larvae can feed on leaves, bore into fruit, flowers or roots, or even be gall-makers. 8mm long.

Labdia sp., **Cosmopterigidae**. Cosmopterygids are about 400 species of often colourful but tiny moths, with elongate delicate bodies. Larvae have broad habits, eating leaves, fungi, and wood, with a few surprising predators.

Goat moth or wood moth, *Endoxyla* sp., **Cossidae**. This family of 200 species of fat, mostly grey/brown species, contains some of the largest and heaviest moths of all. Their larvae burrow in wood and are famous for some being the 'witjuti' grubs eaten by Aboriginal people, especially in the dry interior. This species, from WA, is one of these, with a 170mm wingspan.

143

Leaf-roller moth, *Sycacantha exedra,* **Tortricidae**. This family has more than 1,200 species of varied habits, from rolling leaves for the larvae, to seed, fruit and stem borers. The Codling Moth is a famous pest in this group, although most are harmless like this Qld species, 8mm.

Forester moth or burnet moth, *Pollanisus nielseni,* **Zygaenidae**. This family only has 56 species, but many are very memorable. Many have beautiful deep metallic colours and day-flying habits. This one is from WA, 12mm long.

Cup moth, *Doratifera* sp., **Limacodidae**. The cup moths are named for the shape of the pupal chamber, but are much more famous for their caterpillars, which carry barbs tipped with painful chemicals similar to sea anemone stings. About 115 species of these 'slug-caterpillars' are best avoided.

Sun moth, *Synemon* sp., **Castniidae**. Members of this family are the closest moths to the butterflies, and even their antennae have the tell-tale club shape. The 25 species fly very fast between flowers during daytime. WA, 25mm wingspan.

Plume moth, *Xyroptila marmarias*, **Pterophoridae**. The 40 species of these small moths share the distinctive feature of feather-like wings. Forewings divided into two, and hindwings into three feathery parts. Qld, 16mm wingspan.

Margarosticha repetitalis, **Pyralidae**. This pyralid is a very odd moth. The triangular adults in this group have aquatic caterpillars, feeding underwater on pond plants. Some species even walk underwater as adults to lay their eggs!

Vitessa zemire, **Pyralidae**. Pyralid moths were a large family of 1,200 species with distinguishing features. However the group has been split into two families, with only 200 species remaining in the original classification. Many of these have striking forms in the tropics, as here. 20mm long.

Pygospila tyres, **Crambidae**. The crambids are a new family split from the pyralids, and most are this distinctive triangular shape and have a front-upright sitting stance. More than 1,000 species have varied larval habits but are mainly leaf feeders, often hidden in leaf cases. 40mm wingspan.

Geometridae is a huge family with 2,300 species. Adults have many shapes and often very strong colours, while the caterpillars are often the classic thin, twig-like, leaf-eating loopers or inch-worms.

Comostola cedilla, 18mm across.

Bracca rotundata, from Qld and NSW, 45mm across.

148

Niceteria macrocosma,
from eastern wet forests,
35mm long.

Four o'clock Moth,
Dysphania nomana,
from Qld, 40mm across.

149

Day moth, *Alcides metaurus*, **Uraniidae**. A spectacular species sometimes found in a group, in north Qld, where the caterpillars feed on Euphorbiaceous vines. 60mm wingspan.

Hercules Moth, *Coscinocera hercules*, **Saturniidae**. The 15 species of the emperor moth family punch well above their number. This species is the largest in Australia and nearly the largest in the world. The female shown here is 270mm across – nearly the length of a whole ruler! This giant lives for only a few days as an adult, flying very ponderously in the forests of north Qld.

Above: Emperor Gum Moth,
Opodiphthera eucalypti, **Saturniidae**.
The most widespread of the Saturnids,
found from NT through to Vic.
Colour varies from this beige to a
purple/brown. 70mm across.

Left: *Anthela* sp., **Anthelidae**.
The Athelids are around 100 species
of medium to large moths with rich
colours from yellows to browns.
Their caterpillars are famous both for
being extremely hairy and because
these hairs are tipped with irritating
and sometimes dangerously allergic
chemicals. Best practice in the bush is
never to touch any hairy caterpillars.

Hawk moth, *Agonyx papuana*, **Sphingidae**. The hawk moths are known for their stout, muscular, streamlined bodies, fast flight, and their beauty. They are very important pollinators, sometimes being the only species doing so for a particular flower species. They can hover like hummingbirds, and insert a very long proboscis into deep flowers, some doing so in daytime. 35mm long.

Hawk moth, *Gnathotilbus eras*, **Sphingidae**. Not the most stunning hawk moth, but the most likely of the 60 species to be seen, being found from NT to Vic. It is also one of the few that may be troublesome, as their caterpillars feed on plants in the grape family. 40mm long.

Native Budworm caterpillar, *Helicoverpa (Heliothis) punctigera*, **Noctuidae**.
A serious pest of many crops, from a group of species found all over the world,
which includes names such as army worm and ear worm. They belong to the once
vast family **Noctuidae**, which has now had most of its species transferred to a
nondescript group called **Erebidae**. Adult 15mm long, caterpillar 22mm.

Opposite: Vine Hawk Moth caterpillar, *Theretra latreilii*, **Sphingidae**. This
caterpillar is typical of the whole hawk moth family, which share a simple visible
diagnostic character – the spiky, curved tail on the last segment. East coast, about
40mm long.

153

Speiredonia mutabilis, **Erebidae**. This beautiful blue moth from northern Australia was once a typical member of the **Noctuidae** family, but is now lumped in with visually unrelated groups in the new family **Erebidae**. From Qld, 40mm across.

Fruit-piercing moth, *Eudocima aurantia,* **Erebidae** (Cotacalinae). Once part of the old Noctuid family, these moths are now in the **Erebidae**. They have the amazing habit of penetrating fruit as adults, with a very strong proboscis. In a turnaround from the norm, it is the adults that are pests and not the harmless caterpillars. Citrus and other fruit are spoilt by these moths, Qld, 40mm long.

Tiger moth, *Oeonistis delia,* **Erebidae** (Arctiinae). The tiger moths were once in a distinctive family, the **Arctiidae**, with around 340 species. Today they are lumped into the large **Erebidae** family as a distinctive subfamily. Many have beautiful strong warning colours, advertising that some caterpillars store plant poisons in the adult body. Qld, 25mm long.

Tiger moth, *Amerila rubripes,* **Erebidae** (Arctiinae). This white tiger moth is not just distasteful to potential predators if eaten, it also ejects poisons from its thorax when first disturbed. Found from WA to Qld, 30mm long.

Tussock moth, *Atraxa epaxia*, **Erebidae (Lymantriidae)**. The tussock moths are medium to large and very hairy – both as adults, and more so as larvae. Their caterpillars have characteristic tufts of hair which is particularly irritating and dangerous. There are about 70 species, and again they have recently been moved into the **Erebidae**. Caterpillar 28mm, adult 20mm long.

BUTTERFLIES

In Australia the butterflies comprise six families of what are essentially day-flying moths that share the combined features of clubbed antennae and wings that are not joined in flight by a hook system as in most moths. As there are excellent comprehensive books on the subject, this section is just an introduction to the families.

Wedge Grass Skipper, *Anisynta sphenosema*, **Hesperiidae**. Typical of the skipper family that contains 121 species of these squat, fat-bodied butterflies, which hold their wings in a triangular stance. Their relatively small wings beat very fast, so their flight is faster and more erratic than that of other butterflies. 18mm long.

Orchard Swallowtail, *Papilio aegeus aegeus*, **Papilionidae**. The most commonly seen member of this small but very showy family of 18 species. Male and female have different patterns and the caterpillars start out as bird-dropping imitators, mainly on citrus leaves. This is the female. East coast, 105mm wingspan.

Ulysses Swallowtail, *Papilio ulysses*, **Papilionidae**. The most iconic butterfly in Australia, found along the tropical Qld coast where it is the unofficial emblem. This pose illustrates the largest amount of blue an observer is likely see – beware postcards with fully perfect spread wings, and look for the pin! 90mm wingspan.

Two-spotted Line Blue, *Nacaduba biocellata*, **Lycaenidae**. Typical of the blues, which is the largest butterfly family with 141 species. When at rest, the underside of the wings can be very colourful, and not always blue, but blue tones dominate on the upper side. Breeds on acacia, often attended by ants. Occurs over most of Australia, 18mm wingspan.

Evening Brown, *Melanitis leda*, **Nymphalidae**. Typical of the colours of this family of 81 species. Found in NT and along the east coast. 60mm wingspan. The famous migratory Wanderer butterfly also belongs to this family.

Orange Migrant, *Catopsilia scylla*, **Pieridae**. Typical of the 'whites' family, where yellow species dominate. The most infamous species, though, is the introduced Cabbage White. The Orange Migrant moves around the north from WA to coastal NSW. 50mm wingspan.

WASPS, ANTS AND BEES Order Hymenoptera: 14,900 species

ID: Wasps and ants are an old lineage, with most sharing the body plan of a waist between the thorax and abdomen. The bees are a newer evolutionary line, and do not possess an obvious waist. Most usually with four clear wings, although sometimes only in the sexual castes, as in the ants.

HABITS: All levels of social behaviour can be found in this order, from simple nest-site sharing to complex societies with up to millions of workers and a long-lived queen who supresses their sexual development. Many have an egg-laying organ called an ovipositor, sometimes very long and thin, and in some groups, such as the ants, developed into a sting instead. A few other wasp families, and some bees, share the sting also. Sizes from an incredible microscopic 0.15mm to 120mm.

WASPS

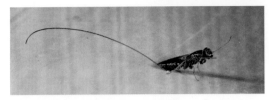

Megalyra sp., **Megalyridae**. A small but very distinctive parasitic wasp family. The ovipositor can be up to eight times as long the body, 100mm all up. This is used to drill through wood to find beetle larvae tunnelling inside, and deposit eggs in them. 4mm body only.

Right: Hatchet wasps, **Evaniidae**, are about 40 species of parasites of cockroach egg cases. The name is from the hatchet-like shape of the waist and small abdomen. 7mm.

Opposite: The sawflies, **Pergidae**, are about 200 species of primitive wasps with no 'waist', and medium-sized stout bodies. Their larvae, which unlike other wasps are leaf-eating grubs, are communal and protected by foul defensive fluids. Many are known as spitfire grubs, waving their tails menacingly when approached. Shown here are an adult guarding her young in the Alpine region, NSW, 16mm, and the spitfires, NSW, 25mm each.

161

Gasteruption sp., **Gasteruptiidae**. This distinctive long abdomen shape belongs to the 140 species of gasteruptid wasps. They are parasites of social wasps and bees. They range in size from 5–85mm – this one is 16mm.

Ichneumon wasp, *Stenarella* sp., **Ichneumonidae**. These wasps are often seen flitting about flowers, between looking for hosts to parasitise. Moths, beetles and other wasps are among a broad list of victims. More than 2,000 species range from 2–120mm long, with the ovipositor up to three times body length.

Braconid wasp, *Callibracon* sp., **Braconidae**. The braconid wasps are 800 species of parasitic wasps closely related to the larger ichneumons. They have a broad list of insect larvae as hosts, from beetles to bugs to other wasps. Some are important biocontrol agents of pest insects. Size range is 1–80mm, and *Callibracon species*, parasites of longicorn beetles, are around 12mm.

Chalcidoidea is a superfamily, a group of about 3,700 species in 20 families in Australia, that best illustrate the myriad of tiny wasps which mainly parasitise insect larvae, eggs and each other – a habit known as hyperparasitism. They average 4mm or less, and include the smallest complex organisms on the planet, at 0.15mm, which are smaller than many single-celled primitive life forms such as amoebas! Here a small selection:

Chalcididae, *Brachymeria* sp., moth parasite, 5mm.

Pteromalidae, *Semiotellus* sp., 2mm.

Eucharitidae, an ant parasite, 3mm.

Eulophidae, *Diaulomorpha* sp., 2mm.

Torymidae, a gall making wasp, 10mm.

Cuckoo wasp, *Stilbum cyanurum,* **Chrysididae**. The cuckoo wasps are 76 species of richly metallic parasites. They invade the nests of larger mud wasps, and deposit eggs of larvae which eat the host larvae. From 2–22 mm – this one 14mm.

Spider wasp, *Cryptocheilus* sp., **Pompylidae**. These wasps stalk spiders and sting them into paralysis, then bury them as food for the wasp larvae. They have curled antennae and the habit of flicking their wings in a hypnotic pattern when approaching a spider. The 231 species reach 35mm, which is the length of the giant species shown here.

Flower wasp, *Hemithynnus* sp., **Thynnidae**. The 750 species of flower wasps are very easy to identify at mating time, when the long-winged male carries the short stout wingless female to flowers for many hours, so she may stock up on sugars for egg production. These eggs then hatch into parasitic larvae, with burrowing beetle and cricket hosts. Male 26mm long.

Velvet ant, *Ephutomorpha* sp., **Mutilidae**. The velvet ants are, like the flower wasps, a family with winged males and wingless females. The 500 species are more diverse in dry regions, and the females are not as diminutive as in flower wasps, but stout bristled insects resembling ants, and possessing a ferocious sting and attitude. Bold colours warn of this danger. WA, 12mm.

Hairy flower wasp, *Campsomeris tasmaniensis*, **Scoliidae**. Part of a family of large, stout and bristled wasps, often boldly coloured, with only 25 species, although often seen on flowers. The extra bristled females dig into wood in search of beetle larvae to parasitise. 25mm.

Paper wasp, *Ropalidia impetuosa*, **Vespidae** (Polistinae). The Paper wasps are 35 species in the subfamily Polistinae of the family **Vespidae**, which also has the potter wasps and the hornets. Shown here is a very typical hanging paper nest under a large leaf. The cells contain larvae and pupae – note the small grub heads waiting for caterpillar food. Adults 14mm.

Paper wasp, *Polistes schach,* **Vespidae** (Polistinae). One of the largest paper wasps in Australia, hunting for caterpillars away from its paper nest. All paper wasps are very painful repeat stingers, mainly when the nest is bothered. 30mm.

Potter wasp, *Delta campaniforme,* **Vespidae** (Eumeninae). With 300 species, the potter wasps are the biggest group within the vespids. Most build some sort of mud nest, free standing in natural and house overhangs, others use existing holes. Their larvae are also fed on caterpillars. *Delta* is a large genus, found over most of the world, with this very long and thin waist. 30mm.

'European Wasp', *Vespula germanica,* **Vespidae** (Vespinae). The hornets are a group of vespids with very bad attitude, responsible for serious stings. Australia was free of this group until the 'European Wasp' accidentally arrived. It makes huge paper nests underground or in home cavities. When not hunting a variety of insects to feed to its larvae, it is attracted to sweets such as soft drinks and cakes, and so easily comes into our space. 26mm.

Mud dauber wasp or digger wasp, *Ammophila* sp., **Sphecidae**. This family contains about 580 species. Many resemble the mud wasps, with very long thin waists. They hunt caterpillars, grasshoppers and more, and dig burrows to house these as food for their larvae. Some use tools such as rocks to tamp down the area afterwards in order to hide the hole. 25mm long.

Hunting wasp, *Cerceris* sp., **Crabronidae**. This family has about 80 species, most quite specialised on a kind of prey to bring back to holes in the ground for their larvae. Leaf beetles, **Chrysomelidae**, are a favourite. 12mm.

173

Sand wasp, *Bembix* sp., **Crabronidae**. Stout-bodied hunting wasps with no obvious waist. They tend to dig holes for their prey in sandy soil, and spend much time hovering searching for ideal sites. Flies are a major source of hosts for the larvae.

ANTS

The 1,300 described species of ants differ from other wasps by having a more complex, one- or two-node waist, and their antennae are elbowed about halfway. The complex caste system involves several types of workers for brood care, nest building and foraging, the soldier caste, and to start new colonies, a winged male and female caste leaves the nest on mating flights. Only some species, such as the bull ants, can sting, and sometimes cause serious allergic reactions.

Bull ant, *Myrmecia nigrocincta*, **Formicidae**. Bull ants are a very ancient Australian lineage of about 90 species. The fearsome jaws are for hunting, but in defence they only hold on, while a sting in the tail injects the severe pain. 25mm.

Meat ant, *Iridomyrmex* sp., **Formicidae**. The aptly named meat ants are fast, organised hunters and scavengers of everything, also quickly sending humans scurrying with their sharp formic-acid nips. Nest groups of up to 300,000 are fully underground, with only a slight mound, and frantic activity above.

Green Tree Ant, *Oecophylla smaragdina,* **Formicidae**. Anyone living in the tropics has run into these ants. They make many small nests of leaves woven together by silk, and hunt and defend very aggressively, locking their jaws in death grips. Unlike other ants, their abdomens and larvae contain a quantity of edible ascorbic acid – Vitamin C – and are eaten by people.

BEES

Before Europeans brought their honey bee to Australia, more than 1,600 species of native bees were doing just fine, pollinating everything. Many different habits exist in these five families, from solitary, to semi-social to fully social. The young are cared for by provision of nectar and pollen and sealed in solitary soil or wood holes, or in various groupings. They collect the pollen, nectar and resins either on hairs on their legs, abdomen, or even in internal crops.

Carpenter bee, *Xylocopa aruana*, **Apidae** (Anthophorinae). The carpenter bees are the largest part of the **Apidae** family of bees, where the European species, *Apis mellifera*, also belongs. They are large, fat, hairy bees which dig holes in soft living and dead wood, to provision a place for their larvae. 20mm

Blue-banded bee, *Amegilla* sp., **Apidae** (Anthophorinae). The blue-banded bees are a small but very noticeable group of bees, which hover frantically between flowers, landing only for split seconds to recover pollen by vibrating the flower, and causing much noise in the process. 14mm.

179

Native honey bee, *Trigona* sp., **Apidae** (Apinae). This group of species – also known as sugar-bag bees, sweat bees and other names – live in tree holes, logs and even house walls, with typical resin tubes as entrances. Up to thousands of these tiny bees share the nest with a similar social structure to 'honey' bees, and make a very nice, more runny honey. 5mm.

Short-tongued bee, *Hylaeus eligans*, **Colletidae**. A family of more than 1,000 species that has coevolved alongside myrtaceous and other Australian lineage plants, and so half the world's species are here. They carry the pollen loads in internal crops, and line their brood cells with a protective polyester-like membrane. The head markings are diagnostic for various species. 10mm.

Rainforest bee, *Palaeorhiza* sp., **Colletidae**. The rainforest bees are a tropical genus of short-tongued bees, usually very boldly and often metallically coloured. They pollinate the many blossoms of the forest canopy.

181

Burrowing bee, *Homalictus* sp., **Halictidae**. About 390 species of burrowing bees nest in the ground, sometimes in colonies, although still as individuals and not a caste. They collect pollen both on the rear legs and on their abdomen hairs. 8mm.

Megachile aurifrons, **Megachilidae**. This small family of 170 species has many names. Some are leaf-cutter bees, cutting out perfect circles from leaves and lining the brood nests with these, others are resin bees or carder bees, lining nests with animal and plant hairs or resins. Pollen collection is on abdomen hairs only, so they are often seen rubbing their underside on the flower. 12mm.

GLOSSARY

ABDOMEN: The rear of the three body divisions of an insect.

ANTENNAE: A pair of jointed sensory organs on the head of all insects; also known as 'feelers'.

APTEROUS: Wingless.

CASTE: One of three or four distinct body forms among social insects, including a reproductive queen, workers, soldiers and reproductive males.

CELL: An area enclosed by veins on wings.

CERCI: A pair of jointed appendages at the tip of the abdomen.

CHRYSALIS: A term used for the PUPA of mainly butterflies and some moths.

CLUBBED: With a swollen, bulbous end. A term applied to the shape of antennae.

COCOON: A silken case which encloses the pupa of several insect groups including many moths.

COMPLETE METAMORPHOSIS: The growth cycle where the young (the larvae) have a different form from the adult, and undergo a pupal stage to become the adult.

DEFLEXED: Pointing downwards.

DETRITUS: Broken-up and usually decaying organic matter.

DIMORPHISM: Differences in the appearance of individuals of the same species, especially between the sexes.

DISTAL: Furthest from the body, e.g. the tip of the wing is the distal part of the wing.

DORSAL: The upper or top surface.

ELYTRA: The hardened forewings that protect the membranous hindwings in beetles (Coleoptera) and are not used in flight.

ENDEMIC: Restricted in distribution to a particular region.

ENDOPARASITE: A parasite living within the body of its host.

EXOSKELETON: The tough, jointed outer covering or skeleton of insects and other arthropods. It is made of chitin; and as it does not grow it has to be shed (moulted) periodically to allow the animal to increase in size.

FILIFORM: Thread-like, a term applied to the shape of antennae.

FRASS: Plant fragments made by wood-boring insects, usually mixed with excreta.

GALL: A growth on plants, often bulbous, caused by the chemical irritation of certain insect groups whose young stages develop inside.

GASTER: The main part of the abdomen in wasps and ants, behind the 'waist' or PETIOLE.

GLOSSA: The mouthparts of bees, also called a 'tongue'.

HALTERES: The club-shaped balancing organs which all flies (Diptera) have in place of the hindwings.

HEMELYTRA (s. HEMEIXTRON): The partly hardened and partly membranous protective forewings of true bugs (Heteroptera) which are still used in flight.

HEXAPOD: Six legged.

HONEYDEW: The sweet secretion of aphids and plant hoppers (Hemiptera) which attracts ants.

HYPERPARASITE: A parasite which parasitises another parasite.

IMAGO: The adult stage of an insect.

INCOMPLETE METAMORPHOSIS: The growth cycle where the young (nymphs) are similar in appearance to adults and develop gradually without a pupa stage.

INQUILINE: An animal living in the nest of another species. In insects, most commonly in the nests of termites and ants.

INSTAR: One stage of growth between moults, from egg to adult, referred to by number. For example a caterpillar may be a third instar or stage caterpillar.

LABRUM: A plate or flap at the front of the head also known as the 'upper lip' because it often partly covers the mouthparts.

LAMELLATE: Pertaining to antennae with fanlike segments at the tip.

GLOSSARY

LARVA (pl. LARVAE): The immature (often grub-like) stage of insects which undergo complete metamorphosis.

LATERAL: Pertaining to the sides.

MANDIBLES: The upper, chewing pair of mouthparts (jaws) of insects, sometimes modified into other shapes.

MEMBRANOUS: Pertaining to wings, the usually transparent flying wings, such as in dragonflies.

MONILIFORM: Bead-like, a term applied to the shape of antennae.

MOULT: To shed the outer 'skin' or exoskeleton in the process of growth.

NYMPH: The immature stage of insects with incomplete metamorphosis life cycle. Nymphs usually resemble the adult except for lacking functional wings which develop gradually on the outside.

OCELLUS (pl. OCELLI): A simple, single-lensed eye present, often in a pattern of three, in many insect groups.

OVIPOSITOR: The egg-laying apparatus of female insects, concealed in some orders, and very long and conspicuous in others, e.g. wasps and crickets.

PALPS/PALPI (s. PALP/PALPUS): Segmented appendages around the mouthparts which are organs of taste and help manipulate food.

PETIOLE: The narrow 'waist' segment of wasps.

PHYTOPHAGOUS: Feeding in or on plants.

PROBOSCIS: Extended mouthparts which are often modified into a tube for sucking. The term is most often used for the coiled tubular mouthparts of moths and butterflies.

PROLEGS: Short appendages on the abdomen of some caterpillars that act as legs. Normal legs are attached to the THORAX.

PROXIMAL: The part of an appendage nearest to the body.

PTERYGOTE: Winged – belonging to the insect orders which are winged (though not all species necessarily have wings).

PUBESCENT: Covered in fine short hair; downy.

PUPA (pl. PUPAE): The usually inactive stage between larva and adult, found in insects with a COMPLETE METAMORPHOSIS life cycle.

RAPTORIAL: Adapted for seizing and holding prey, like the forelegs of praying mantids.

ROSTRUM: The beak-like piercing and sucking mouthparts of all bugs (Hemiptera). Also applied to the 'snout' of weevils.

SAPROPHAGOUS: Feeding on decaying organic matter.

SCAPE: The first (basal) and often largest segment of the antenna.

SCLERITE: Any one of the separate plates making up the SEGMENTS of the EXOSKELETON.

SCLEROTISED: Hardened (or armoured) like the ELYTRA of a beetle, compared to the soft tissue of, for example, caterpillars.

SEGMENT: A division of the EXOSKELETON, between flexible joints in the body and appendages.

SERRATE: Saw-like or tooth-like, a term applied to the shape of antennae.

SETA (pl. SETAE): A stiff bristle-like hair.

STRIDULATION: Production of sound by rubbing two parts of the insect body, usually a toothed file on legs or wings. The varied calls of grasshoppers and crickets are all created this way.

TARSUS (pl. TARSI): The insect 'foot'; the last of five divisions of the leg, and itself divided into one to five segments.

TEGMEN (pl. TEGMINA): The toughened, leathery forewing of several orders, especially Orthoptera, Blattodea and Mantodea.

THORAX: The middle of the three major body divisions of an insect between head and ABDOMEN. The legs and wings are attached to the thorax.

TYMPANAL ORGAN: A stretched drum-like membrane which forms the ears of insects like grasshoppers and others.

VENTRAL: On the underside of the body.

VESTIGIAL: Only partly developed, small and non-functional.

VIVIPAROUS: Bearing live young.

INDEX

191